# CARESSING THE CREED

*Reflections on the Apostles' Creed*

## Richard Allen Farmer

WESTBOW
PRESS®
A DIVISION OF THOMAS NELSON
& ZONDERVAN

Scripture taken from the New King James Version. Copyright © 1979, 1980, 1982 by Thomas Nelson, Inc. Used by permission. All rights reserved.

WestBow Press books may be ordered through booksellers or by contacting:

WestBow Press
A Division of Thomas Nelson & Zondervan
1663 Liberty Drive
Bloomington, IN 47403
www.westbowpress.com
1 (866) 928-1240

ISBN: 978-1-5127-2397-7 (sc)
ISBN: 978-1-5127-2398-4 (e)

Library of Congress Control Number: 2015920525

Print information available on the last page.

WestBow Press rev. date: 01/15/2016

# Contents

# Foreword

Since January 1, 2014, it has been my joy to serve as pastor of the Crossroads Presbyterian Church in Stone Mountain.

I love to preach, and I have not lost my love *for* and commitment *to* the discipline of research, writing, editing, praying over, and delivering expositions of Scripture. What a joy it has been to prepare spiritual food for the saints at Stone Mountain. They are a most receptive congregation with whom it is my joy to worship, week after week.

For fifteen weeks of my first year, I preached my way through the lines of the Apostle's Creed, which we recite at least once a month in our morning worship experience. I offer these sermons so that we are reminded of what we believe and that to which we hold.

I am grateful to the congregation that journeyed with me as I mused on this historic doctrinal statement.

To them, the Crossroads Presbyterian Church family, I fondly dedicate this book.

Richard Allen Farmer
Stone Mountain, GA
April 2015

# Chapter 1

# I Believe in God the Father Almighty

Text: Genesis 17:1–8; 2 Corinthians 6:14–18

Trinity Sunday is celebrated on the Sunday after Pentecost. On that day we celebrate, and we specifically celebrate the Trinity—God the Father, God the Son, and God the Holy Spirit. In some churches they recite the Athanasian Creed. That creed is named after Athanasius, who was a fierce champion of orthodox faith. The Athanasian Creed reads as follows:

> Whosoever will be saved, before all things it is necessary that he hold the Catholic Faith. Which Faith except everyone do keep whole and undefiled, without doubt he shall perish everlastingly. And the Catholic Faith is this, that we worship one God in Trinity and Trinity in Unity. Neither confounding the Persons, nor dividing the Substance. For there is one Person of the Father, another of the Son, and another of the Holy Ghost. But the Godhead of the Father, of the Son and of the Holy Ghost is all One, the Glory Equal, the Majesty Co-Eternal. Such as the Father is, such is the Son, and such is the Holy Ghost. The Father uncreated, the Son uncreated, and the Holy Ghost uncreated. The Father

Incomprehensible, the Son Incomprehensible, and the Holy Ghost Incomprehensible. The Father Eternal, the Son Eternal, and the Holy Ghost Eternal and yet they are not Three Eternals but One Eternal. As also there are not Three Uncreated, nor Three Incomprehensibles, but One Uncreated, and One Incomprehensible. So likewise the Father is Almighty, the Son Almighty, and the Holy Ghost Almighty. And yet they are not Three Almighties but One Almighty.

So the Father is God, the Son is God, and the Holy Ghost is God. And yet they are not Three Gods, but One God. So likewise the Father is Lord, the Son Lord, and the Holy Ghost Lord. And yet not Three Lords but One Lord..)

Without apology, we are Trinitarians. We believe that God has made Himself known in three distinct yet equal persons—God the Father, God the Son, and God the Holy Spirit.

When we recite the Apostles' Creed, we take on each of those persons in a section. I want to take a first look at what we are saying when we profess our belief in God.

In this first line, there is both a description of God in a specific role and a statement about one of His attributes. The specific role is *father*. The attribute is *omnipotence*.

## God as Father

Before we look at God as a father, let's first examine the phrase "I believe." Belief can be quite nebulous and nonspecific. I remember singing a popular song in our middle school choir. It was written in 1953, and it was terribly general. The song spoke of believing but never fully stated the object of the belief.

Some people have a theology like this. It is general enough to cover all bases, and it doesn't nail you down to a specific position or belief. The Apostles' Creed is designed to articulate not simply that we believe in God. We believe in a specific God who has come to us in Jesus Christ. The creed will then proceed to name names and make it clear that we're not talking about a general, ambiguous deity here.

Actress Shirley MacLaine writes in her book *Out on A Limb,* "Not that I am God, but that we are god, that all is god, that we're all part of a cosmic oneness. And if we don't feel that we're god, that's simply because we're ignorant. And the only way that we can banish our ignorance and discover our godness is by enlightenment that will come through meditation."

When some people say, "I believe in God," they really mean, "I believe in me, for I am god." They might mean, "I believe in a higher power," or they may want to say, "I believe there is a force out there and up there."

People of the Christian faith, who have named Jesus the Christ as their only Savior and Lord, don't see themselves as gods. No, we are in an increasingly intimate relationship with the God of heaven and earth, the God of the Scriptures, and the God of creation.

I believe in God the Father. This idea suggests potential intimacy.

Do you remember the plaintive words from Papa God to Israel through the prophet Malachi in Malachi I? "A son honors his father, and a servant his master. If I then am the father, where is my honor? And If I am a master, where is my reverence?" (NKJV)

To say God is our Father is to say there is a relationship that has been established and there is a growing, ongoing intimacy between this Father and His child. That is the presupposition of our OT text. Abram is being addressed by the one who identifies Himself as the covenant maker. He will enter into an intimate relationship with Abram. He will work in Abram's life. In addition, the Father will cause Abram to become a father of many nations (verse 5). Papa God changes Abram's name and his present. He changes Abram's outlook and his future (verses 6–7). In our NT lesson, Paul says that the ability to make good decisions about those with whom we align ourselves is based on our relationship with God. If we are temples of the living God and God dwells in us, then we will not yoke ourselves to those for whom this is not true. Note the creedal phrase in verse 18, "I will be a Father to you. And you shall be My sons and daughters, says the Lord Almighty."

Are you a child of God? Can you say with confidence that God is your Father? That only happens through spiritual adoption.

In his book *The Apostles' Creed*, Stuart Briscoe tells the story of staying with a family in New England. The family had two daughters who looked quite different from each other. One daughter said, "My sister is the natural child of my parents, but I was adopted." Briscoe asked how she felt about that. The daughter replied, "Oh, they just *had* her, but they *chose* me" (Briscoe 2010 p. 28).

Have you responded to the fact that the Father has chosen you and called you out of sin and into a new life with Him?

*I believe*—Such belief ought to be centered around something and someone specific.

*In God the Father*—This means there is a growing relationship.

*Almighty*—This is to say this God is like no other.

## God as Almighty

When we speak of the attributes of God, there are two categories—*communicable* and *incommunicable*.

Communicable attributes of God are those that He has shared with humanity in some form. God is loving, and we may be loving. God is forgiving, and we may forgive one another. God is love, and we have the capacity to love. These traits of God have been communicated to us or shared with us. Incommunicable attributes (traits) are those that God has reserved for Himself. God is all-knowing. We are not. God is everywhere at the same time (omnipresent). We are not. God has all might. We say, "He's almighty." But we are not.

I believe in a named, specific God who functions in my life as Father. That Father has all power in Himself.

> "He is almighty" is something that cannot be said of any human, earthly father. However, it can be said of our God. A child at various ages may say the following: At four years old, he or she may say, "My daddy can do anything." At seven years old, he or she may say, "My dad knows a lot, a whole lot." At eight years old, he or she may say, "My father doesn't know quite everything." At twelve years old, he or she may say, "Oh, well, naturally Father doesn't know that either." At four years old, he or she may say, "Father? Hopelessly old-fashioned." At twenty-one years old, he or she may say, "Oh, that man is out-of-date. What did you expect?" At twenty-five years old, he or she may say, "He knows a little bit about it but not much." At thirty years old, he or she may say, "Maybe we ought to find out what Dad thinks." At thirty-five years old, he or she may say, "A little patience. Let's get Dad's assessment before we do anything." At fifty years old, he or she may say, "I wonder what Dad would have thought about that. He was pretty smart." At sixty years old, he or she may say, "My dad knew absolutely everything!" At sixty-five years old, he or she may say, "I'd give anything if Dad were here so I could talk this over with him. I really miss that man."

> —Ann Landers, *Wake Up and Smell the Coffee!* (New York: Villard, 1996)

With God as our Father, we never go through those periods. He never seems smarter and then not so smart and then smart again. He never changes. Would you welcome this God as your Father Almighty?

Amen.

# Chapter 2

# Maker of Heaven and Earth

Texts: Genesis 1:1–2:3; Hebrews 1:1–2

When we recite the Apostles' Creed, we state that we believe. We are not shallow or ambiguous in our belief. We believe in someone very specific. We believe in (and have confidence in) the Father who has all might.

The creed goes on to state that this God is the maker of heaven and earth.

This is not a sermon on creationism versus evolution. I shall not in this sermon bring up Charles Darwin, Bill Nye the Science Guy, or Ken Ham.

I do not wish to debate the statement that God is the maker of heaven and earth. We hold to the authority of Scripture. The Bible does not offer creation as a theory. It is stated as a fact (Genesis 1:7–8, 10), so I receive it as such.

The newest addition to my vocabulary is the word *polysyndeton*. It is a literary device that I have heard, read, and even used, but I didn't know the term for it. Polysyndeton (meaning "bound together") is the stringing together of conjunctions for artistic and literary effect. For instance, in Joshua 7, we read the account of the punishment of Achan, who took some loot from a raid and hid it among his own possessions. He was killed for his disobedience and dishonesty. In Joshua 7:24 (KJV), we read, "*And*

Joshua, *and* all Israel with him, took Achan the son of Zerah, *and* the silver, *and* the garment, *and* the wedge of gold, *and* his sons, *and* his daughters, *and* his oxen, *and* his asses, *and* his sheep, *and* his tent, *and* all that he had: *and* they brought them unto the valley of Achor."

The list is given a great rhythm and effect through the use of the polysyndeton. That device is also used here in Genesis 1. A commentary I consulted while I was working on this text noted that there are almost a hundred *and*s in Genesis 1. This narrative of the creative power and activity of Papa God has a flow that is almost musical.

There is no attempt here or in our NT lesson to defend God or prove His existence. The creation is stated as an assumed reality. This reads as a fact, not as an offering of one of several equally valid viewpoints.

Some fancy themselves to be creative or generative. We can dream up ideas and generate new ways of tackling a problem. Technically, however, we don't create. We merely rearrange existing ideas, entities, structures, and thought patterns. Our peerless God, however, creates out of nothing. The Latin phrase is *ex nihilo.* There are three Hebrew words used in connection with the creation of humanity. *Asah* means to make. *Yatsa* means to form. *Bara* means eto create. Only *God* does that. When we recite the Apostle's Creed, we are saying we believe that origins lie in the hands of our God. While this short phrase, "Maker of heaven and earth," simply speaks of creation, I wonder if we might also affirm our responsibility to take care of the earth. God created the heavens and the earth and then gave to Adam the privilege of caring for the earth (Genesis 1:28–2:15). Perhaps to say that we believe in the Father Almighty who made the heavens and the earth is to also cooperate with Him in keeping the earth. Maybe we should conduct ourselves in such a way that it couldn't be said, "God *created* the earth, and then humans *trashed* it."

The creed has us articulating a belief (confidence) in the God who has all might, who has all creative power, and who is Lord over all the earth as its Creator. We are to elevate and deify no person, no academic inquiry, no republic, no municipality, no language, no denomination, and no institution. It is interesting that Genesis 1 does not say, "In the beginning the heavens and the earth were formed." The description is not passive but active. In the beginning *God* created.

If this phrase is true, then we must acknowledge God as the Lord of both heaven and earth. Many will accept the fact that God rules heaven. They don't want Him ruling earth!

Let me suggest three lenses through which we might view and appreciate this phrase from the creed.

## 1. Origins

While this has become a contentious subject, it need not be. The text says that God created every creature after its kind" (Genesis 1:24–25). That suggests that creatures (both animals and humans) were not created in a primitive form and then they evolved into something else. The implication of the text is that they were created in a fully formed fashion. Humans were created after their kind. Apes were also created after their kind. One did not evolve into the other.

## 2. Ownership

According to Psalm 24, the earth is the Lord's. He founded it and established it. To say God is the maker of heaven and earth is to acknowledge that the earth has an owner.

Maltie Babcock (1858–1901) was a pastor in Lockport, New York; Baltimore, Maryland; and, lastly, New York City in the late nineteenth century. He was physically fit and liked to run. Often when he'd go for a run, he'd say to his colleagues, "I'm going out to see my Father's world." He penned this poem, which is found in many hymnals.

1. This is my Father's world and to my listening ears
All nature sings, and round me rings the music of the spheres.
This is my Father's world: I rest me in the thought
Of rocks and trees, of skies and seas;
His hand the wonders wrought.

2. This is my Father's world. The birds their carols raise.
The morning light, the lily white, declare their Maker's praise
This is my Father's world. He shines in all that's fair.
In the rustling grass I hear Him pass;
He speaks to me everywhere.

3. This is my Father's world. O let me ne'er forget
That though the wrong seems oft so strong, God is the
ruler yet.
This is my Father's world. Why should my heart be sad?
The Lord is King. Let the heavens ring
God reigns: let earth be glad

To say in the creed, "I believe in God, the Father Almighty, maker of heaven and earth," is to say, "I know this is my Father's world." This part of the creed is both a call to environmental sensitivity and a reminder of the handiwork of our God! This brings me to the third lens.

## 3. Stewardship

Maybe you and I ought to adjust our behavior in light of this great statement. If God has made the heavens and made the earth, what might He expect of those of us who populate the earth? *Oh, Pastor Farmer, don't go New Age on us. We don't want to hear about water conservation and recycling and carbon emissions and land usage and issues of sustainability.*
I don't want to think about those issues either. I wouldn't have to give such a moment of thought if this was *your* world or *my*

world. I'd just let it simply destroy itself, and that would be the end of it all. But this is Papa *God's* world. *He* is the maker of heaven and earth, says the creed.

May I suggest some action steps? Plant a garden at your house or secure a plot in a community garden. Use reusable bags when you go grocery shopping. Don't litter. I saw a man lay a Styrofoam cup on the ground outside his car at a restaurant and then get in his car. I picked the cup up and asked him to take it with him.

Not too long after that, I saw a lady open her car door at a light and put an entire cake, in its plastic dome, on the ground and drive away. *Don't litter.*

Here is Cecil Alexander's nineteenth-century poem that was later set to music.

> Refrain
> All things bright and beautiful,
> All creatures great and small,
> All things wise and wonderful:
> The Lord God made them all.
> 1. Each little flower that opens,
> Each little bird that sings,
> He made their glowing colors,
> He made their tiny wings.
>
> Refrain
>
> [Most hymnals omit the following verse]
>
> 2. The rich man in his castle,
> The poor man at his gate,
> He made them, high or lowly,
> And ordered their estate.
>
> Refrain

3. The purple headed mountains,
The river running by,
The sunset and the morning
That brightens up the sky.

Refrain

4. The cold wind in the winter,
The pleasant summer sun,
The ripe fruits in the garden,
He made them every one.

Refrain

5. The tall trees in the greenwood,
The meadows where we play,
The rushes by the water,
To gather every day.

Refrain

6. He gave us eyes to see them,
And lips that we might tell
How great is God Almighty,
Who has made all things well.

Refrain

Take care of this planet. The Lord God, Father Almighty, made it all. Our response to environmental problems is a *theological* one. We take care of all things bright and beautiful *because* our God is the maker of heaven and earth.
Amen.

# Chapter 3

# And in Jesus Christ, His Only Son, Our Lord

Text: Luke 6:46–49

This passage begins with a haunting question regarding motive. It is clear that both in Jesus' day and ours, many are attracted to Him. They found His rhetoric disturbing, His actions dramatic, and His personality compelling. The danger then and now is that we could simply be attracted to the personality of Jesus but never fully give ourselves to His teaching. One could stand around the edge of a relationship with Jesus, all the while enjoying only the experience of being around Him.

Some young adults live with their parents and never quite learn independent living skills. We call that *failure to launch.* Some infants never quite learn to take the nipple when they are breast-feeding. We call that *failure to latch.* Some Christians never learn to bow to Jesus the Christ as their only Master. We call that *failure to submit.*

This phrase of the creed has us articulating three truths about Jesus.

- Jesus is the Christ—the Messiah, the expected one, the Anointed One. In OT times there were three offices to which one could be anointed—prophet, priest, and king. Jesus was all three.

- Jesus is God's only Son. Literally the word describing Jesus means "one of a kind." He was not created as other sons are. Rather, Christ is *begotten* of the Father. Christ is of the same nature, the same genetic material, the same essence as that of God!
- Jesus is our Lord.

It is that third item that causes many to stumble. Why call Jesus Lord if we have no intention of submitting?

God has made Jesus both Lord *and* Christ (Acts 2:36). What does it mean to call Jesus Lord? Some want Jesus as their Savior but not as their Sovereign Lord. They want Him as Redeemer but not as ruler. They welcome the one who is holy but not the one who is the Godhead. The foundation of a solid Christ-honoring life is obedience. That's what we build on. We must never confuse flowery words with faithful ways or platitudes with practices. Fine rhetoric is no substitute for compliance. To say, "Jesus is Lord," is to say that Christ reigns and that we will bow to that reign. The Greek word for Lord (*kurios*) can be translated as "sir, master, husband, owner." The rabbis taught the doubling of a name showed affection (as in "Lord, Lord" in Luke 6:46; "Martha, Martha" in Luke 10:41; and "Abraham, Abraham" in Genesis 22:11).

We could express affection for Jesus by saying, "Lord, Lord" but fail to obey Him! The parallel passage to this text is Matthew 7:24–27. Only the gospels of Luke and Matthew contain this parable. Note that the difference between the two house builders is not that one heard the words of Jesus and the other didn't. No, the difference is in hearing *and doing* (Luke 6:47) and hearing *and not doing* (Luke 6:49). We could attend a worship service three times a week and be part of a small group and study the Bible an hour a day. However, if that does not lead us to also *obey* Christ, it is hollow. To say, "I believe in Jesus, His only Son, our Lord," is to acknowledge and embrace the idea of submission, wherein we do what Jesus says and obey what Jesus commands.

Peter T. Forsythe was right when he said, "The first duty of every soul is to find not its freedom but its Master."

A.W. Tozer says that people who are crucified with Christ have three distinct marks.

1. They are facing only one direction.
2. They can never turn back.
3. They no longer have plans of their own.

In his autobiography, *A Life in Our Times*, John Kenneth Galbraith illustrates the devotion of Emily Gloria Wilson, his family's housekeeper.

> It had been a wearying day, and I asked Emily to hold all telephone calls while I had a nap. Shortly thereafter the phone rang. Lyndon Johnson was calling from the White House.
>
> "Get me Ken Galbraith. This is Lyndon Johnson."
>
> "He is sleeping, Mr. President. He said not to disturb him."
>
> "Well, wake him up. I want to talk to him."
>
> "No, Mr. President. I work for him, not you."

She did not wake her boss. That's obedience. Is that you? Is that me? We pray so.

Amen.

# Chapter 4

# Who Was Conceived by the Holy Ghost, Born of the Virgin Mary

Text: Isaiah 7:14; Matthew 1:18–25

Don Kenyon was my professor of Bible studies at college. In one of his comments about the incarnation of Christ (Christ being born as a human), Don Kenyon said something that struck me. He said, "Mary did no more than any of us should do. She made herself available to God for His use." Our Roman Catholic brothers and sisters put Mary in a much higher position. Professor Kenyon was closer to the teaching of the gospels. Mary is not to be worshipped. Rather, she is to be admired for yielding herself to God's purposes. Mary was a virgin when she became pregnant with Jesus. Some traditions teach that Mary remained a virgin her entire life (perpetual virginity). Some say that Mary herself was born without sin (immaculate conception). These positions, however, are not in the Bible.

Note verse 18 of our NT text. Matthew notes that the child in Mary's body is of the Holy Spirit. Note verse 20. When the angel speaks to Joseph, the angel says that the child in Mary's body is of the Holy Spirit. Note Luke 1:35. After Mary ponders her virginity and the impossibility of having a baby, the angel tells Mary that what is happening in her body is directly due to the Holy Spirit overshadowing her. In fact, in verse 16 of our NT lesson, Matthew wants to make it clear that Joseph is not the genetic father of Jesus Christ. No man's role as a husband is mentioned until verse 16. The phrasing "of whom" in verse 16 is singular feminine. It indicates that Jesus was born of Mary, not of Mary and Joseph. *This is no ordinary birth and no ordinary man.*

*When the Holy Spirit is at work in us, expect the impossible, the illogical, the unexpected.* Given that Papa God is almighty and we affirm that attribute in the creed, we are reminded that God could have saved us without this human gift. Papa could have spoken from the heavens, and we would have been saved. However, in His plan God sent Himself in human form. *The emphasis here in the text is not on Mary but on the work of the Holy Spirit.*

The conception of the Christ was important. It established the fact that this is God's doing. No human—not Mary or Joseph—could take credit for this. The birth of Christ to a virgin is important. It establishes the purity of Christ. The psalmist says that we were conceived in sin (Psalm 51:5), but Jesus was not. The fact that Mary was virginal until she was impregnated by the Holy Spirit means that Christ was completely sinless not only in character but in the very way in which He was delivered to us.

To say we believe in Jesus, who was conceived in a unique way and born through a virgin woman, is to say we affirm the *otherness* of Jesus. He is one of a kind. We don't understand Christ strictly from a biological point of view. He transcends biology and logic.

In his book *Miracles*, C. S. Lewis writes, "In Science we have been reading only the notes to a poem; in Christianity we find the poem itself." Professor Alva McClain of Grace Seminary has said, "A sinless man is a greater miracle in the moral order than the virgin birth in the biological.

| As God | As Human |
|---|---|
| He is worshipped. | He worshipped |
| He was called God. | He was called man. |

| | |
|---|---|
| He was called Son of God. | He was called Son of Man. |
| He is prayed to. | He prayed to the Father. |
| He is sinless. | He was tempted. |
| He knows all things. | He grew in knowledge. |
| He gives eternal life. | He lays down His life. |

All of the fullness of divinity dwells in Him. He has a human, mortal body. In the creed we articulate our belief in the Christ who, while equal with the Father, was sent through the Holy Spirit and through a yielded peasant named Mary. This is a statement about our salvation. Clearly Jesus was both human and divine. He was both man and Messiah. In the highest validation of our human condition, God sent Himself to earth as a baby. Hebrews 4 says that we don't have a high priest who cannot relate to our infirmities. In all points He experienced our human condition, except that He never sinned (Hebrews 4:15).

I recently watched a documentary titled *The Flat*. Arno Goldfinger, the narrator and writer, has the task of cleaning his recently deceased grandmother's apartment in Tel Aviv. As part of learning more about his grandmother's past, Goldfinger and his mother travel to Germany. In a cemetery they search for his great-grandmother's grave. His mother says she is not moved by any of this. Goldfinger asks, "Does it bother you that you aren't moved?" She says, "I can't say if it bothers me or not." Her son then says, "It bothers *me* that you aren't moved by what we're seeing here."

Reader, if you're not moved by this great truth of Scripture, it bothers me. Should we not celebrate that our Lord Christ was unlike any other in His conception and birth, in His life and death and resurrection? He was conceived by the Holy Ghost. Wow! He was born of a virgin. Wow!

Amen

# Chapter 5

# Suffered under Pontius Pilate, Was Crucified, Died, and Was Buried

Text: Isaiah 53:1–9; Matthew 27:11–14, 45–60

I celebrate the multicultural composition of the congregation I serve. At Crossroads Presbyterian Church, we have congregants from at least twelve different countries. We are not *tolerating* the differences. We are *celebrating* them. There is quite a bit of difference between those two postures—toleration and celebration. Some people think that in order to embrace a person of another cultural, ethnicity, or religious tradition, one must get rid of any absolutes. Rather than do that, we gather around a common creed. We do not hesitate to state what we believe. There are three ecumenical creeds, which are held by every Protestant denomination and our Roman Catholic and Orthodox colleagues—the Apostles' Creed, the Nicene Creed, and the Athanasian Creed.

Some people say it is confining to box ourselves in with a creed. "Let's be open to all traditions and opinions," they say. Others say we don't need a set of beliefs that drive us. We merely need to do good work on the earth. "Deeds, not creeds. Acts, not facts," they say. I want to suggest that we need both a commitment to a solid, biblical set of creedal statements that motivates us *and* a commitment to flesh those statements out.

This OT passage has such beautiful word pictures in it. Warren Wiersbe, commenting on Isaiah 53, says that when God made the universe, He used His fingers (Psalm 8:3). When He delivered Israel from their Egyptian captors, He used His strong hand (Exodus 13:3). But to save lost sinners, says Wiersbe, God had to bare His mighty arm (Isaiah 53:1).

Clearly the one described in Isaiah 53 is the Christ. At the same time, he is both the root and the offspring of David (Revelation 22:16). Christ is the humble root out of dry ground, the tender plant, the rejected one, the smitten and afflicted one (vs. 1–5). He is the one who, when reviled, does not retaliate (v. 7). When he stands before Pilate and the accusations fly, Christ says nothing (Matthew 27:12–14). When He stood before Caiphas, He was silent (Matthew 26:62–63). Luke 23:9 says that when Jesus stood before Herod Antipas, He was silent. I want to offer five descriptions as a way of processing this part of the creed.

### Humiliation

This is the voluntary condescension of the Christ. He suffered under Pontius Pilate. This refers to Christ's humiliation in a court on manufactured charges. That suffering was both physical and emotional. Christ suffered so that when you and I suffer, He can relate to us. Have you ever been subjected to humiliation that was leveled against you simply because you were old or young, black or white, American or African or Caribbean, short or tall, slender or overweight? When you suffer in any way, Christ understands. All kinds of accusations were leveled against Him (Matthew 27:12–13, 17–18, 22–23).

### Expiation

The prefix *ex* means "out of" or "from." Expiation refers to the act of taking our sins away (John 1:29). Then after they mocked Him (Matthew 27:31) and spit on Him (Matthew 27:30) and struck Him on the head (Matthew 27:30), they crucified Him (Matthew 27:35).

## Propitiation

The prefix *pro* means *for*. This is the act of appeasing a wrathful God. God's wrath is not merely satisfied. Through the act of propitiation, God's wrath is turned into favor (Romans 3:23–26).

Oswald Chambers says,

> We trample the blood of the Son of God if we think we are forgiven because we are sorry for our sins. The only explanation for the forgiveness of God and for the unfathomable depth of His forgetting is the death of Jesus Christ. Our repentance is merely the outcome of our personal realization of the atonement that He has worked out for us. It does not matter who or what we are; there is absolute reinstatement into God by the death of Jesus Christ and by no other way, not because Jesus Christ pleads, but because he died. It is not earned, but accepted. Our Lord does not pretend we are all right when we are wrong. The atonement is a propitiation whereby God, through the death of Jesus, makes an unholy man holy.

He died. He didn't simply faint. He died. This, however, is not the death of an ordinary human. No, this is the death of the unique Son of God, who was conceived by the Holy Ghost and born of the Virgin Mary. We are Trinitarians. We believe that God has revealed Himself as Father, Son, and Holy Spirit. In a sense, this is not about the death of Jesus only. This is the one God in three persons, giving of Himself to satisfy His own judgment.

Christ's substitutionary death satisfied the wrath of God so that when Papa looks on us, it is propitious and favorable. There's an old legend that says death and the grave had a chat one day.

The grave said to death, "Let's get Jesus." The grave said to death, "You bring Him down, and I'll hold Him." He died. Death grabbed Jesus and delivered Him to the grave. But the grave could not hold Him.

When Jesus died, He was fulfilling His purpose (Mark 10:45). He was buried. It sounds so final. Yet that is not how the narrative of Christ's life on earth ends. But for some, it is. You have buried Christ and think you don't have to deal with Him anymore.

Billy Sunday said, "If you live wrong, you can't die right."

## Reconciliation

You and I were alienated from Papa God. Christ brought us back to the God from whom we came (Colossians 1:21–22)

## Anticipation

When this Crucified One is buried, that is not the end of the story. There is more to come (Matthew 17:22–23; 26:26–29).

Amen.

# Chapter 6

# He Descended into Hell. The Third Day He Rose Again from the Dead

Text: Ephesians 4:7–9; 1 Peter 3:18–20

Since the eighth century, the church has been reciting what has eventually come to be known as the Apostles' Creed. We are unapologetic about being a creedal people. The alternative is to state nothing that clearly summarizes what we believe.

The first phrases of the creed present no problem. They are clear and biblical. We *do* believe that God is Father and Creator of both heaven and earth. We *do* affirm that Jesus Christ is Lord and is God's only Son. We believe that Christ's conception and birth were unique. According to both the Scripture and the creed, He was conceived by the Holy Ghost and born of the Virgin Mary. He *did* suffer under Pontius Pilate. He *did* experience humiliation, agony, and crucifixion, and He was buried. All those phrases are also in Scripture, and they present no problem.

Now with the phrase "He descended into hell," we hit our first wall. While the phrase "He descended into hell" is in the creed, it is not in the Scriptures. There are eight passages in which the presence of Jesus in *hell* or *the place of departed spirits* is referenced, including Acts 2:27, Romans 10:6–7, Ephesians 4:8–10, Philippians 2:9–11, Revelation 5:13, and John 5:25. The seventh and eight passages are in 1 Peter 3:18–20 and 1 Peter 4:6.

An excerpt from the Westminster Confession:

> The bodies of men, after death, return to dust, and see corruption: but their souls, which neither die nor sleep, having an immortal subsistence, immediately return to God who gave them: the souls of the righteous, being then made perfect in holiness, are received into the highest heavens, where they behold the face of God, in light and glory, waiting for the full redemption of their bodies. And the souls of the wicked are cast into hell, where they remain in torments and utter darkness, reserved to the judgment of the great day. Beside these two places, for souls separated from their bodies, the Scripture acknowledges none.

Some interpreters have said that "He descended into hell" suggests that Christ went to hell to preach to the spirits who were there. One view says that Jesus went to hell to preach to those who were disobedient during the building of the ark and to give them a second chance. Nowhere else in Scripture are we told of this second chance *after* death. Another view is that *spirits in prison* refers to demonic spirits or Old Testament believers who didn't have the opportunity to express faith in the coming Messiah while they were living. This view is comforting but not biblical. Peter does not tell us the content of Christ's proclamation.

Christ didn't preach a second chance for salvation to unbelievers in Hades. He didn't preach salvation to fallen angels, for angels cannot receive salvation. He didn't preach evangelistically to OT believers. In a third option, some have said that the phrase "He descended into hell" simply shows the depth of His death. The idea is that He went all the way down to death. Alister McGrath points out that there was a great difference between being raised *from death* and being raised *from the dead* for New Testament writers. Jesus was raised *out of those who are dead.*

With other expositors, I believe that Christ went *by the Spirit* to imprisoned people and proclaimed His victory, His triumph. In the first century, when a general or a king won a victory, a herald would go before the king or general and announce his victory. After the announcement and pronouncement of victory, the creed says, He rose from the dead. This is the celebration part of the creed. Death is the most feared of enemies. First Corinthians 15:26 says that the last enemy that will be destroyed is death. Jesus Christ handled the last enemy by dying …*and rising.*

Jesus remained in the grave Friday and all day Saturday. Then the grave lost its grip on Jesus (Acts 2:24). The old preachers say, "But early, I said early, Sunday morning, He got up!" The swoon theory, which was put forward by H. E. G. Paulus in 1828, says that Christ merely fainted. The soldiers took Him down and buried Him alive. The spices in which He was wrapped and the cool temperature of the tomb revived Him. An earthquake rolled the stone away, and Christ walked out of the tomb. No, the executioners of that day certainly knew when a person was dead and when a person was not. Christ got up from the grave, and He was not dazed or confused.

"Pastor Farmer, why is the resurrection important? What's in it for me?" some of you might ask. I'm glad you asked. I offer three benefits of a firm belief in Christ's rising from the dead.

- It affirms the divinity of Jesus (Romans 1:4).
- It affirms the power of Christ to forgive sin (1 Corinthians 15:17).
- It affirms Christ's power over the last enemy, death itself (Romans 6:9). Since we are in Christ, if death has no dominion over *Him,* it has no dominion over *us.* (See 1 Corinthians 15:12–20 for six items that would be directly affected if Christ had not risen.)

You are reading the writings of a man who was, as a teenager, very afraid of death. I have loved Jesus Christ since I was twelve years old. I knew where I was going when I died. That was not the problem. I had recurring nightmares that I'd be conscious in my casket, and I pictured myself banging on the lid, trying to get out. I imagined being lowered into the ground and hearing the shovels of dirt hit the lid of my casket. I was greatly helped by a remark from D. L. Moody (1837–99) of Northfield, Massachusetts.

Some day you will read in the papers, "D. L. Moody of East Northfield is dead." Don't you believe a word of it!
At that moment I shall be more alive than I am now;
I shall have gone up higher, that is all,
out of this old clay tenement into a house that is immortal
a body that death cannot touch, that sin cannot taint;
a body fashioned like unto His glorious body.
I was born of the flesh in 1837.
I was born of the Spirit in 1856.
That which is born of the flesh may die.
That which is born of the Spirit will live forever.

Once I read that and the clear promises of Scripture, my fear was gone. At best, if my body should be laid out for viewing, you could only say, "Here lies the shell. The nut has gone home."

Ralph Douglas West of the Church Without Walls in Houston, Texas, said, "If there is no resurrection, we should leave the church and go to the synagogue and eat the Seder meal. If Christ is not raised, then up is down and down is up. If Christ is not raised, right is wrong and wrong is right. If Christ is not raised, north is south and south is north."

Christ rose with such power that Paul had to write rhetorical questions in response. "O Death, where is your sting? O Hades (grave), where is your victory."

Christian Gellert's eighteenth-century hymn says,
1. Jesus lives, and so shall I.

Death! thy sting is gone forever!
He who deigned for me to die,
Lives, the bands of death to sever.
He shall raise me from the dust:
Jesus is my Hope and Trust.

2. Jesus lives, and reigns supreme,
And, his kingdom still remaining,
I shall also be with him,
Ever living, ever reigning.
God has promised: be it must:
Jesus is my Hope and Trust.

3. Jesus lives, and by his grace,
Vict'ry o'er my passions giving,
I will cleanse my heart and ways,
Ever to his glory living.
Me he raises from the dust.
Jesus is my Hope and Trust.

4. Jesus lives, I know full well
Nought from him my heart can sever,
Life nor death nor powers of hell,
Joy nor grief, hence forth forever.
None of all his saints is lost;
Jesus is my Hope and Trust.

5. Jesus lives, and death is now
But my entrance into glory.
Courage, then, my soul, for thou
Hast a crown of life before thee;
Thou shalt find thy hopes were just;
Jesus is the Christian's Trust.

Amen.

# Chapter 7

# He Ascended into Heaven and Sitteth on the Right Hand of God, the Father Almighty

Text: Colossians 3:1; Hebrews 7:20–25; Acts 1:9–11

When some were children, they were given the opportunity to receive Christ as their Savior and Lord. When the person leading the child to a commitment would ask, "Where is Jesus now?," the child would answer, "In my heart."

Technically such a question has three correct answers. Christ is (1) in our hearts, (2) present in all the earth, and (3) in the heavens at the right hand of God the Father.

I want to celebrate all three realities and work on the last one a bit through this text in Hebrews 7.

*Christ is in our hearts.* The Scriptures teach not only that Christ inhabits the whole earth but that individuals may have such a relationship with Him that it can be said, "Christ lives in my heart: (Ephesians 3:17; Colossians 1:27).

*God, in Christ, fills the whole earth* (1 Kings 8:27; Psalm 139:7–12).

*Christ is at God's right hand.* But when did He get there? He arrived immediately after His ascension. And what precisely is He doing there? He is our Advocate (1 John 2:1; Romans 8:34). The Greek word for *advocate* is *parakleetos*. The word means "called alongside." An *advocate* is anyone called to assist another. It is used by attorneys who plead the case of a person on trial. Only five times is this noun used in the NT. Four times it is used in John 14–16 and translated as *Comforter*, when Jesus used that noun to describe the Holy Spirit.

Christ pleads our case before the Father God. Our case is against Satan, the accuser of the brethren (Revelation 12:10). If we had no Advocate, we'd be accused of sinful deeds by the Accuser, and we'd have to defend ourselves. We would fail miserably. Prophets take God to the people. A priest takes the people to God. Christ is our priest and Advocate. He takes us to stand before the judge, and He defends us. He tells the Father that we are guilty, but there is a twist in Christ's advocacy. He stands at the bench and declares our guilt and then takes our guilt upon Himself so that we may be declared righteous and free!

In this short yet packed verse of Hebrews 7, we have two distinctive works of Christ highlighted. He saves, and He intercedes. He saved us from our sin, from ourselves, and from the evil Accuser by dying in our places on the cross. He then went back to heaven, from where He had come. He now intercedes for us. Christ's first act, saving us, was a once-and-for-all act at Calvary. The second act, His intercession, is ongoing. The first act was for all humanity. This second act is only for those who come to God through Jesus (verse 25).

To use aquatic imagery, Christ saw us drowning. He picked us up and saved us. He then put us back in the water, and now He swims alongside us.

To use legal imagery, Christ stood with us at our trial. He agreed with the judge that we were guilty. On the basis of His sacrificial death, we were then declared free, and He walked out of the courtroom with us. He continues to plead our cases.

To use maritime imagery, we were shipwrecked and floating along with no signs of being recovered or rescued. He got in the water *Himself* and pulled us to Himself. He had pity on us. He now intercedes for us.

To use pugilistic imagery, Christ saw us in the ring, getting the life beaten out of us. He came and stopped the fight, took us to His own corner, dressed our wounds, put salve over the cuts on our eyebrows, retaped our hands, and sent us back out to fight. Now, however, He goes with us and is *in* us and fights *for* us.

I know you've heard jokes about lawyers, but this is a good Advocate. I am glad Christ died. His death was the beginning of my life. However, it is a grave error to think of Him as dead. Christ is risen! He is risen indeed! He is risen just as He said!

Hebrews 7:25 says of Christ, "He ever liveth," or, "He always lives." He's alive right now. What does this mean for you and me?

*Christ's present intercession on our behalf at God's right hand frees us from trying to be good people.* We can't achieve some high moral state on our own. The good news is that we don't even have to try. Christ forms His life in all those who receive Him. Every day He is at God's right hand, taking on the case against us. That means *we* don't have to plead our cases daily.

*Christ's present intercession on our behalf at God's right hand frees us from trying to save ourselves.* A key text of the several that address this is Hebrews 1:3, which says, "Who being the brightness of His glory and the express image of His person, and upholding all things by the word of His power, when He had by Himself purged our sins, sat down at the right hand of the Majesty on high."

*Christ's present intercession on our behalf at God's right hand is a statement of Christ's authority.* A person with no authority could not go to God's lofty throne and sit down. This is what drives our outreach, our mission, even our worship. Christ has all authority in heaven and on earth (Matthew 28:18). John Stott says, "Only because all authority on earth belongs to Christ dare we go to all nations. And only because all authority in heaven as well is his have we any hope of success."

Where is Jesus the Christ now? He is in our hearts. He is in all the earth. He is at God's right hand, serving as Advocate. In this very sacred space, there stands a living Christ who wants to embrace you and save you and turn your life around. He ascended into heaven. That's the language used in the ascension text in Acts 1. *Lest people think some switcheroo might take place, Luke says the same one that went up is the one that shall come down.* It was this same Jesus, who healed the lame, unstopped deaf ears, raised Lazarus from the dead, canceled the funeral procession for a young man from Nain, and gave sight to the blind. This same Jesus! He gave hope and healing to a hemorrhaging woman and courage to the fear-ridden. This same Jesus. He worked wonders on a withered hand. This same Jesus. He walked on water and commanded the winds and the waves to stop acting up and behave themselves. This same Jesus. He came down to save. He went up to intercede. He came down in humility. He went up in triumph. He had power then, and He has power now at the right hand of God the Father. He shall come back in power too! For now He is at the right hand of God. From thence He shall come to judge the quick and the dead, but that's for the next chapter.

Amen.

# Chapter 8

# From Thence He Shall Come to Judge the Quick and the Dead

Text: Psalms 7:11; 75:4–7; John 5:24–30

Our creed speaks of the past deeds of Jesus Christ. He *was* conceived by the Holy Spirit. He *was* born of the Virgin Mary. He *did* suffer under Pontius Pilate. He *was* crucified. He *was* buried. He *did* rise from the dead. He *did* ascend to heaven. Then the creed speaks of Jesus' present. He is presently sitting at the right hand of God (Hebrews 7:25). Now we address a line in the creed that speaks of Christ's future. He is now at God's right hand, and from there (thence) He *shall come* to judge the quick (living) and the dead.

Many people believe that God will judge no one. They believe that God is a God of love only. Such persons cannot conceive of a God who would allow anyone to go to hell. They cannot imagine that at the end of time, there would be anything but one big love fest, if there is anything at all. What does it mean to recite this line that says that Christ will come *and* judge both the living and the dead?

When I graduated from high school, I was planning on going to college, I was the organist of a large interdenominational choir in New York City. Some of the members of that choir were from a church that believed that the second coming of Christ was imminent. They believed that Jesus was coming again to earth very soon. I believed, as the Scriptures teach, that no one knows the day or the hour of Christ's coming. One of my colleagues in that choir said, and I quote, "Richard, we don't have time to go to college. Jesus is coming soon." I told her, "If He comes soon, He can pick me up at college. If He doesn't come, I will have a college degree."

Our primary text (John 5) contains clear teaching about the end of the world and some of the events connected with that time. If we hold to the authority and the veracity of Scripture, then this passage will not be dismissed.

Those of us who have received Jesus Christ as Lord and Savior, who follow Him and define ourselves as *Christians* need not fear the end. When we recite, "From thence He shall come to judge the quick and the dead," we do not tremble. That's because of verse 24. We have passed from spiritual death to spiritual life and need not fear the judgment. Before we look at the rest of this passage, let me remind you of this same teaching in Paul's Corinthian letter (2 Corinthians 5:10–11; Romans 14:10).

The judgment of God will be of two types and to two groups. First there are *those who have done good.* This refers not to some superior moral standing. Rather, these people have embraced the Lord Jesus. They made good choices. They said yes to Christ and yes to God's offer of salvation. They confessed their sins. They gave over the reins of their lives to Christ's control. We who have embraced Christ will be judged, but that judgment is more a standing before our God, who sees us *in* Christ. We are then acquitted and proceed to a resurrection of life (verse 29).

Then there are *those who have done evil.* This is the group of people who have said no to Christ and no to God's offer of salvation. They will proceed to a resurrection of condemnation (verse 29).

I can hear some cry, "Unfair, unfair!" I can hear some say, "I am a good person. I help people whenever I can. I have given thousands of dollars to the United Way. I was a Boy Scout. I was a

Girl Scout. I helped elderly people across the street. I volunteered at my local hospital. I tutored youngsters so that they could keep up academically. I helped the local library when they had their book sale. I should not be condemned." Others will ask, "How can one reconcile a loving God with judgment and fire and hell and eternal punishment?"

God owes us no explanation of His ways. William Barclay, a Scottish theologian and expositor, has suggested that there are many reasons God may judge humanity (The Apostles' Creed For Everyman. p. 201ff).

- For failure to respond to human need (Luke 16:19–31).
- For leading others into sin (Matthew 18:3–7).
- For professing faith without practicing it (Matthew 7:21–23).
- For embracing materialism without regard to spiritual need (Luke 12:13–21).
- For refusal to repent (Luke 13:1–5).

Christ shall come to judge the living and dead. That may be understood both literally and figuratively. Literally, when He shall come, all those in the grave will hear His voice, and we are alive and remain shall be caught up to meet Him (1 Thessalonians 4:13–17). Figuratively, those who are spiritually alive and those who are spiritually dead shall be judged.

Because we are hidden in Christ, we need not fear this coming judgment. Christ, indeed, shall come to judge the living and the dead. But we who know Him are not dreading the meeting. He shall say to us, "Come, you blessed of my Father, inherit the kingdom prepared for you from the foundation of the world" (Matthew 25:34).

Amen.

# Chapter 9

# I Believe in the Holy Ghost

Text: Ezekiel 36:22–32; John 14:15–18, 25–26

Thomas Lindberg writes that Norwegian explorer Roald Amundsen was the first to discover the magnetic meridian of the North Pole and to discover the South Pole. On one of his trips, Amundsen took a homing pigeon with him. When he had finally reached the top of the world, he opened the bird's cage and set it free. Imagine the delight of Amundsen's wife back in Norway when she looked up from the doorway of her home and saw the pigeon circling in the sky above. No doubt she exclaimed, "He's alive! My husband is still alive!"

So it was when Jesus ascended. He was gone, but the disciples clung to His promise to send them the Holy Spirit. What joy when the dovelike Holy Spirit descended at Pentecost. The disciples had with them the continual reminder that Jesus was alive and victorious at the right hand of the Father. This continues to be the Spirit's message.

We believe in the Holy Ghost. However, two pertinent questions would include the following: Who is the Holy Spirit, and what does He do?

## The Identity of the Holy Ghost

Note that the Holy Spirit is a person. The Holy Spirit is referred to as He, not it (John 15:16, 17). There is an old foot-stomping gospel song that says, "I got it. I got it. I got it. I got it. Something about the Holy Ghost I just can't explain, but I got it." We are Trinitarians who believe that God has expressed Himself in three distinct, equal persons. If that is true, you cannot describe the Trinity as God the Father (He), God the Son (He), and then God the Holy Spirit (It). No, we see the Holy Ghost as person. Look at John 16:13. Just before we examine why the Holy Spirit came and we celebrate His activity in our lives, note that He is spoken of as if He has a personality. We are not speaking of some impersonal force here or some power that makes you shake or fall out on the floor or speak in unintelligible languages. We are speaking of God in the form of the Spirit. In John 14:16, when the Spirit is spoken of, Jesus says He will send to us *another* helper. There are two Greek words for *another*. *Allos* means another of the same kind. *Heteros* means another of a different kind. The Greek for *another* in John 14:16 is *allos*, "another of the same kind." So we don't have a Spirit coming who is different in substance from the Father and the Son. He is as they are.

## The Role of the Holy Spirit

What is His role in the believer's life?

- He comforts or helps the believer (John 14:16).
- He takes up residence in the believer (John 14:17).
- He will teach the believer (John 14:26).
- He will remind the believer of what Jesus said and taught (John 14:26; 15:26).

Occasionally you'll hear of a Holy Ghost rally or a Holy Spirit conference. The Holy Spirit Himself would probably not endorse an event in which He would be highlighted. The Holy Spirit comes to turn the spotlight on Jesus! "He will convict the world of sin, righteousness and judgement" (John 16:8–11). "He will guide the believer in truth" (John 16:13). "He will glorify Jesus" (John 16:13).

Note again that He doesn't push Himself as much as He puts the spotlight on Jesus the Christ. As important as the work of the Holy Spirit is in guiding, teaching, sanctifying, and helping the believer, He is never to usurp the place of Christ in our thinking. The Spirit Himself wants us to think of Christ. The Spirit testifies of Christ (John 15:26).

The Spirit of God produces in us the fruit of Christlike character so that we may be authentically Christian. I believe in the Holy Ghost. I believe a relationship with Him is necessary if I am to live a life that honors, glorifies, and points to Christ. Not every person can know this relationship with the Holy Ghost of which Jesus speaks in John 14–16.

Another name for the Holy Spirit is the Spirit of truth. Note that this relationship with the Holy Spirit is not universal. Look at John 14:17. The world (those apart from Christ) cannot receive Christ *because* (1) they don't see Him (see John 3:3, which says, "Unless one is born again, he cannot see the kingdom of God") and (2) they don't know Him (see 1 Corinthians 2:14, which says, "The natural man does not receive the things of the Spirit of God, for they are foolishness to him; nor can he know them, because they are spiritually discerned").

We have looked at the identity of the Holy Spirit (as a person). We have looked at the role of the Holy Spirit in the believer's life. I offer a declaration and a question. I believe in the Holy Ghost! Do you?

Amen.

# Chapter 10

# I Believe in the Holy Christian Church

Text: Psalm 22:22, 25; Matthew 16:13–19

Some years ago a British politician named Lord Boothby wrote a book titled *What I Believe*. In it he wrote, "The history of the Christian churches has been one of atrocious cruelty. All of them have done untold harm to the world. The traditions of the Christian churches for centuries can be summarized as dogma, persecution, secession, hatred, destruction, and fire. In fact, everything that Jesus loathed and denounced."

Some people's understanding and opinion of the church is all negative. They see the church as clunky, too political, too bureaucratic, and irrelevant. As for us, we want to love what Jesus loved. He loved the church and gave Himself for it. We who follow Jesus ought to love what He loved. How can you love Jesus and hate His bride (Ephesians 5:25)?

Over the past thirty years, I have had the privilege of traveling internationally and seeing many iterations and configurations of the church. I have seen or heard about, especially in international settings, Christians doing relief work as a way of getting embedded in a culture or a geographical area that is not open to traditional mission work. This question comes to me every time I am in such a setting, "What sets the church apart from a dozen other agencies that build housing, dig wells, and start orphanages and schools?

What sets us apart from the Peace Corps or UNICEF? What marks us as the body of Christ? What are we doing or saying that *only* we are doing or saying?" I want to suggest three questions that we who follow Jesus the Christ raise and no other agency does. They are the marks of the church. I believe in the holy Christian church. It does have its problems, but it an organism that God uses to transform the world. The creed uses the phrase "I believe in the holy Catholic church." The word *catholic* simply means *universal.* The Greek word *katholikos* means "according to the whole." To say, "The church," is to refer to its relevance across the ages. I believe in the church that can reach the person of the first century and the twenty-first.

Opinions on Jesus's identity varied as much in the first century as they do today. In Matthew 16, Jesus questions His disciples about what they are hearing out in the marketplace and in the streets. They begin to offer what they've heard. In Matthew 14:1–12, we read of the decapitation of John the Baptist. Some believed that Jesus was John who had risen from the dead. Others believed that Jesus was not the Messiah. Rather, he was Elijah, the forerunner who would tell of the Christ who was to come (Malachi 4:5). Although Mark and Luke contain this account, only Matthew says that one of the identities people thought of was Jeremiah. Jeremiah was the first of the latter prophets and was known for his authority and his weeping. Some saw that combination in Jesus and linked Him to Jeremiah. There were many other prophets known to this first-century population, and some of them likened Jesus to one of those (verse 14). Jesus is not content to allow these disciples to simply quote others.

This question comes to all of us from our Lord Christ: "Who do *you* say I am?" The *you* is emphatic and plural.

*Let me raise this as the first question a maturing church must answer. Who is Jesus?* Is He simply a good teacher? An exemplary moral man? A miracle worker? A good listener and Counselor? Reliever of human suffering? Who *is* He? A group of people who refuses to grapple with this question is not worthy to call itself a church!

Simon Peter answers for the group, as he does often (Matthew 15:15–16; 19:25–28; 26:40). The late George Gardiner said that when we get to heaven, we will know Peter. He will be the one with the foot-shaped mouth. In a one-liner, Peter floats an answer to this significant question. His answer, while short, is robust. "You are the Christ." That is, Christ is the long-awaited fulfillment of prophetic utterance. He says Jesus is "the Son of God." You are in a unique relationship with the Creator. Finally he says Jesus is "the living God" ". Peter is saying, "You are the son of the God who is not dead, as are the other deities."

Don Kenyon was one of my most memorable Bible professors at Nyack College. One morning we entered the classroom, ready to take a final exam in New Testament survey. We had learned the basic outline of every book in the New Testament, and we were prepared to write about what we knew. Don Kenyon went to the board and said, "Ladies and gentlemen, the final exam will consist of one question. I want it answered on one side of one piece of paper. He wrote on the board, "Who is Jesus Christ?" Kenyon then said, "If you don't know the answer to that question, you don't know the New Testament."

Who is Jesus to you? It is fine to quote others, but after some time you ought to have your own clear testimony.

A young preacher just starting out, Gregory would fill his sermons with quotations from philosophers, theologians, and politicians. Gregory seemingly had every other paragraph beginning with Socrates said this and Plato said that and Winston Churchill said this. Finally an old man in the back stood up and said, "That's fine, son, but what do *you* say?" The first question is a question of *identification*. Who is Jesus?

The second question is as follows: *From where does your insight come?* Verse 17 contains a glowing commendation and affirmation for Peter. Jesus says that Peter is correct and that mere mortals could not have given him such an insight. Flesh and blood could not have revealed (uncovered) this truth. I want to suggest that a goal of us all should be *to live down here and listen up there.* We want to walk on earth and yet have our ears tuned to the heavens. God is speaking, and some will have such spiritual vitality that they will hear Him. A maturing church takes its orders from on high. It receives its mandates from the God who is still speaking. If you only listen to the prevailing culture, you will only proclaim the secular and carnal. If we listen to the God who speaks, we will proclaim truth and do so with power and authority.

What a statement Peter has made. Much has been made about where this puts Peter. He is to be revered, some say, because of what he has just uttered. Our Roman Catholic colleagues teach that Peter was the first bishop of Rome and that all his successors have Christ-given authority and infallibility. Peter is the small stone (*petros*). Christ is the bedrock, the foundational stone, the chief cornerstone. It is clear in this text that *Jesus* is the builder of the church, not Peter (Matthew 16:18).

The foundation of the church, according to Ephesians 2:20, is the teaching of the apostles and prophets, but Christ is the chief cornerstone of the church.

Peter is receiving his information from a source other than the overheard conversations in the market. The Christ, who reveals Himself, still speaks and urges us, like Peter, to have our ears attuned to what heaven is saying. Upon the rock of sound prophetic utterance and clear apostolic teaching, Christ is building his church. *The first question is one of identification. The second question is a question of revelation.*

Do you remember the campaign with the slogan "Got milk? The phrase was created by the advertising agency Goodby, Silverstein & Partners. In an interview in *Art & Copy,* a 2009 documentary that focused on the origins of famous advertising slogans, Jeff Goodby and Rich Silverstein said that the phrase almost didn't turn into an advertising campaign. According to a *New York Times* piece, "People at Goodby, Silverstein thought it was lazy, not to mention grammatically incorrect." The advertisements would typically feature people in various situations involving dry or sticky foods and treats such as cookies. The person then would find him or herself in an uncomfortable situation because of a full mouth and no milk with which to wash it down. At the end of the commercial, the character would look sadly to the camera and boldly displayed would be the words, "Got Milk?"

The third question is this: *Got keys?* Peter has demonstrated such maturity here that Jesus gives to him and to all disciples the keys.

For a few years of my childhood, my siblings and I were latchkey kids. Our mother worked, and we got home from school before she got home from work. For a while we had to go to a neighbor's house when we got home from school. Then came the day when I got my own key to our apartment. It was on a chain around my neck. It wasn't a fancy or ornate key, but it represented authority and the trust of my mother. My dear colleagues in ministry, I know *you* trust *God*. Hear this good news. God trusts *you!* So much so that He gives you the keys of authority to be used responsibly in kingdom work. This matter of *binding* and *loosing* in verse 19 has caused some confusion. It is not true that we get to dictate what God will do. I have heard people say that if you pray in faith, God *must* answer and grant your request. I have heard people teach that you can command the heavens to open and pour out blessings. But no. As we mature, we learn what is on the heart and mind of God, and *we* will what *He* wills. The better understanding of verse 19 is this: Whatever you bind on earth *will have been bound* in heaven, and whatever you loose on earth *will have been loosed in heaven.* As we agree with God, we will only bind what He would bind and will only loose what He would loose.

Peter would use those same Christ-given keys to open the door of faith to Jews (Acts 2), Samaritans (Acts 8), and Gentiles (Acts 10).

Who is Jesus? He is the Son of the living God. What is the source of your information and inspiration? Not flesh and blood but the God in heaven who still speaks. What is the source of your authority? You have the keys, given by the loosing, binding God, who trusts us to do what he would do.

Actor Kevin Bacon recounted the time when his six-year-old son saw the movie *Footloose* for the first time.

> He said, "Hey, Dad, you know that thing in the movie where you swing from the rafters of that building? That's really cool. How did you do that?
>
> I said, "Well, I didn't do that part—it was a stuntman.
>
> "What's a stuntman?" he asked.
>
> "That's someone who dresses like me and does things I can't do.
>
> "Oh," he replied and walked out of the room, looking a little confused.
>
> A little later he said, "Hey, Dad, you know that thing in the movie where you spin around on that gym bar and land on your feet? How did you do that?"
>
> I said, "Well, I didn't do that. It was a gymnastics double."
>
> "What's a gymnastics double?" he asked.
>
> "That's a guy who dresses in my clothes and does things I can't do." There was silence from my son. Then he asked in a concerned voice, "Dad, what *did* you do?"
>
> "I got all the glory," I replied.

We function in the earth by doing what God would do if He were here in the flesh. We bind, we loose, we proclaim, we alleviate suffering, we encourage, we admonish, we rebuke, we love, we serve. I can picture some angel asking God, "How did you do that?" God answers, "Oh, I didn't do that. Those are my doubles on the earth. They are called the church." The angel asks, "What *did* you do? I hope *He* says of *our* work, "I got all the glory.

Amen.

# Chapter 11

# (I Believe in) the Communion of Saints

Text: 1 Corinthians 1:2

Some of the language of the church is unique to us, and it is little understood by those who are not lovers of God through Christ. Paul writes to the saints in Corinth. Every week, in the weekly pastoral letter to the congregation I serve, I address them as the saints at Stone Mountain. Many outsiders can't imagine we call one another saints. Most people would be very deferential and say sheepishly, "Well, I ain't no saint."

Joe: "My mama's a saint."
Mo: "Yeah, a Saint Bernard!"

But who are the saints? In the Roman Catholic tradition, a saint is a person who lived a holy life and is now in heaven. In a somewhat democratic process, the candidate for sainthood is nominated by the people, and the church studies his or her life. Then the candidate needs to accomplish two miracles, presumably from heaven, to demonstrate divine power and favor. Next come the beatification and canonization ceremonies.

In the Protestant tradition, of which we are a part, saints are normal Christians. We can be called the saints while we are living on the earth. The word *saints* does not imply perfection. It is a term of identification. In Greek, the word for *saints* is *hagios*. It is translated as *holy.* Without apology, we are the holy people, imperfect as we are.

*Being a saint is a calling. We are called to God.* Note these verses.

- Romans 1:7 says, "To all who are at Rome, beloved of God, called to be saints."
- Second Corinthians 1:1 says, "To the church of God which is at Corinth, with all the saints who are in all Achaia."
- Ephesians 1:1 says, "To the saints who are in Ephesus, and faithful in Christ Jesus."
- Philippians 1:1 says, "To all the saints in Christ Jesus who are in Philippi."
- Colossians 1:1 says, "To the saints and faithful brethren in Christ who are in Colossae."

When we give our hearts and lives to Jesus Christ through the confession of sins, we are called to His family. We are *called* to be saints. That calling is both a calling *from* as well as a calling *to.* We, the saints, are people called *from* darkness to light, *from* death to life, *from* sin to salvation (1 Corinthians 6:9–10). Then Paul says, "And such were some of you." But God called the Corinthians and you and me to Himself. We have turned our backs on the old life and said yes to a transforming Christ.

*Being a saint is a calling. We are not only called to God. We are called to community.* Saints live in community. That's what makes this Christian life difficult. If we could be on our own and serve in isolation, we might have an easier time. However, Papa has given us one another! In the New Testament, the singular *saint* is used one time (Philippians 4:21). Every other time the word appears in the plural. Whether we like it or not, God has given us the community of saints.

Perhaps you've heard this poem.

To live above with the saints we love
Ah, that will be glory.

To live below, with the saints we know?
Well, that's quite another story.

To say, "I believe in the communion of saints," is to state our confidence in the idea and ideal that what God does in the earth, He accomplishes through His church, the communion (community) of saints. There are some people who profess love for Christ but not His church. How can you not love what He loves? There is a verse in Hebrews that serves as a reminder to all who profess to love Jesus. Hebrews 10:24–25 says, "And let us consider one another in order to stir up love and good works, not forsaking the assembling of ourselves together, as is the manner of some, but exhorting one another, and so much the more as you see the Day approaching." We who are called to God in Christ are at the same time called to community!

In 1971, Stephen Gaskin and four hundred hippies from the San Francisco area settled in Summertown, Tennessee, and they started "the Farm." That communal family still exists today. Down from 1,500, the 160 people who live there share their goods with one another. They live in a cooperative, shared community bound together by principles commonly held—care for the environment, simple living, freedom from materialism and conspicuous consumption.

I believe that we, the communion of saints, make more of an impact on our world as a communion of saints than we ever do as individuals. What would happen if we took the *idea and ideal* of community seriously (Acts 2:41–47; 4:32–37)? The English word *fellowship* in Acts 2:42 is from the Greek word *koinonia*. It refers to an intimate bond, a communion. A growing community of saints will serve one another, share with one another, lean on one another, learn from one another, and follow hard after God with one another.

When I was in college, Tom Skinner came to preach in our chapel. When he started speaking about community, he asked our student body of six hundred, "How many of you know a student who had to leave school because of finances?" Many of us raised our hands. Then he asked, "Why didn't you each give that person two dollars?" There is such power in our effectiveness as a collective. As a community, we can accomplish significantly more than we could as individuals.

The communion of saints is diverse. The communion is comprised of Blacks, Caucasians, Asians, Native Americans, very wealthy people, middle-class earners, and people in abject poverty.

Little Samantha got lost. She ran up and down the streets of her town but couldn't find any landmarks to give her directions home. Confused and now crying, Samantha was found by a policewoman. The officer stopped to help and put her in the front seat of her police car. They drove around and looked at the area until Samantha saw her church. She pointed to it and said to the policewoman, "You could let me out now. There is my church, and I can always find my way home from here."

If left to ourselves, you and I will not find our way home, but if we can see the church, the community of saints, as our landmark, we can go from there. We are in an ongoing permanent communion with Christians who have gone on before us. This community of saints is both viable and invisible.

The final stanza of the hymn, "The Church's One Foundation" reads as follows:

Yet she on earth hath union with God the Three in One
And mystic sweet communion
with those whose rest is one
Oh, happy ones and holy
Lord, give us grace that we
Like them, the meek and lowly,
On high may dwell with Thee.

Amen.

# Chapter 12

# (I Believe in) the Forgiveness of Sins

Text: Psalm 32:1–5; 1 John 1:5–10

This is the second of the so-called penitential psalms (Psalms 6, 32, 38, 51, 102, 130, and 143), and it is the lectionary reading for Ash Wednesday. It is thought to have been written by David after his adulterous affair with Bathsheba and his arranging for her husband's murder.

## 1. The Beatitude of Self-Awareness

The first psalm opens with a beatitude. It pronounces blessing on the person who does not walk in the counsel of the ungodly. The first psalm says that happiness attends those who do not stand in the path of sinners. However, not everyone lives such a life.

This thirty-second psalm has a beatitude as well. Blessed is the person who is a sinner and *knows* she or he is a sinner. Only when one is self-aware can one be forgiven. When we confess to God that sin/those sins of which we are aware, we are forgiven. Our sin is then covered—not covered *up* but covered, as in *taken care of*. Sin is variously defined as missing the mark, rebelling against God and His law, and wandering from the moral or ethical path laid out by God.

Forgiveness can be variously defined as the lifting of a burden, the canceling of a debt, and the changing of one's status in the eyes of a judge.

## 2. The Consequences of Silence and Denial

David suggests that there are physiological consequences when one does not confess sin or repent of rebellious action. Verse 3 of our psalm describes those physical manifestations of silence in the face of sin. It is impossible to escape the judgment of the God who made us and who expects a distinctive life from us. David says that he was keenly aware of God's hand on him. The hand of God is both heavy and light. God's hand is heavy when we are in rebellion. God's hand is light as He, after our confession, relieves us of the burden of sin and the weight of our rebellion. Let's turn our attention to the epistle of 1 John.

## 3. The Danger of Duplicity

In the movie *The Mirror Has Two Faces,* one character says to the other, "There are two things I don't like about you—your face." Are there two sides to our faces? Do we say we have fellowship with God, who is the Light, and then actually walk in darkness? Do we say we are in union with the one who is the truth but actually fail to *practice* the truth?

## 4. The Big If

Look at 1 John 1.
"But if we walk in the light … (verse 7)
"If we confess our sins … …(verse 9)

Sin presents darkness all around. Rebellion causes aches in the bones and groaning all day long. Wandering from God's path leads to the draining of vitality from one's being. But … we believe in the forgiveness of sins. We believe that Papa God can give us a new start. To recite this line from the creed, "I believe in the forgiveness of sins," is to say we believe one does not have to remain in darkness, rebellion, or sin. In Christ, God offers us a new walk.

David told us about the consequences of a life in which sin goes unaddressed and unconfessed. What are the results if one confesses sin? Forgiveness (Psalm 32:5). Unbridled joy (Psalm 32:11).

We could sum up this psalm by turning to Proverbs 28:13, which says, "He who covers his sins will not prosper. But whoever confesses and forsakes them will have mercy."

Amen.

# Chapter 13

# (I Believe in) the Resurrection of the Body

Text: 1 Corinthians 15:35–56

**1. The Body Is an Instrument of Good and Evil ... Simultaneously.**

The body is the vehicle/conduit through which we honor God (1 Corinthians 6:13b–20). A compelling reason to take care of the body is that it is the instrument through which we serve God's purposes. Greeks believed that all matter was evil. Anything material was, therefore, evil. This created a problem with Jesus' incarnation. A perfect God, the Greeks thought, would not take up residence in something as evil as a human body. Note the warning in Romans 6:12–13, where the Christian is reminded that we have at least two options for using our bodies. We may glorify our God with (through) our bodies. We can also use those same bodies as instruments of unrighteousness.

Without being fanatical, I am committed to taking care of my body. I am not a vegetarian or a vegan, but I am committed to a fitness regimen. I tell people that I treat my body like a rental apartment. I want it to be in such good shape when I turn it in that I get my deposit back. First Corinthians speaks of the body being sown—that is, put into the ground or returned to the earth.

My friend Archie lost a significant amount of weight. When I asked him how he did it, he said, "Well, the Bible says our bodies are the temples of the Holy Spirit, but I was becoming a cathedral."

## 2. The Body Is a Deteriorating Instrument.

Our bodies are wearing out. That need not be a distressing thought. That realization might make us live more intentionally. Paul argues that a seed doesn't sprout until it first goes into the ground and dies (1 Corinthians 15:36). We have these natural bodies that are slowly declining. They are but temporary containers and conduits. Someone has described the seven ages of a human as follows: spills, drills, thrills, bills, ills, pills, and wills.

One day the body shall completely wear out, and you shall return that body to the dust (Ecclesiastes 12:7). At the same time, the spirit of the person goes to God (2 Corinthians 5:8). Our bodies are instruments used for good and evil, and they are declining daily. If we end here, that's quite depressing.

## 3. Those Bodies Are Redeemable.

One day we shall have new bodies (Philippians 3:21; 1 John 3:2; 2 Corinthians 5:1). Upon death, the body goes into the ground or to a crematorium. The body and spirit then are rejoined when the Lord returns (John 5:28–29; 1 Thessalonians 4:13–17). Some ask, "What about those who die in fires or are cremated or die in an explosion? They have no bodies to be raised." God, who has all power, will handle that.

New bodies? Jesus had one (John 20:19–20). Jesus had unusual properties in His resurrection body. Jesus could pass through closed doors (John 20:19). Jesus could appear and not be recognized (Mark 16:12). Jesus could suddenly appear (Luke 24:36).

What may be said of these new bodies we shall have? They will be the opposite of the bodies we have now.

- Sown in dishonor, raised in glory (v. 43).
- Sown as a natural body, raised as a spiritual one (v. 44).
- Sown as corruptible, raised as incorruptible (v. 53).
- Sown as mortal, raised as immortal (v. 53).
- Sown with cancer, raised cancer-free.
- Sown with coronary disease, raised with no heart problems of any kind.
- Sown with speech impediments, raised with ability to clearly proclaim.
- Sown in frustration, raised in confidence.
- Sown in fear, raised in courage.

In his letter to the saints at Rome, Paul calls this the redemption of the body (Romans 8:18–23). We used to sing a chorus that I haven't heard for a long time. It's based on 1 Corinthians 15:52–53.

We shall be changed.
We shall be changed,
Changed from mortal to immortality
In the twinkling of an eye.

To say, "I believe in the resurrection of the body," is to be reminded of our frailty *and* of God's promise to change our bodies. To recite this line from the Apostles' Creed is to articulate a non-anilhilst view of life. That is, we don't believe that upon death we are annihilated. We believe something else happens after death. We do not believe that death is final or that the grave is the last stop. I believe that our bodies do not stay in the grave. I believe in the resurrection of the body. To recite this line of the creed is to articulate the promise of God. To say this is to articulate hope. This motif of getting up from the grave is the essence of the gospel (1 Corinthians 15:1–4, 14).

In one of his lighter moments, Benjamin Franklin penned his own epitaph. He didn't profess to be a born-again Christian, but it seems he must have been influenced by Paul's teaching of the resurrection of the body. Here's what he wrote: "The Body of B. Franklin, Printer. Like the Cover of an old Book Its contents torn out, And stript of its Lettering and Guilding, Lies here, Food for Worms, But the Work shall not be wholly lost: For it will, as he believ'd, Appear once more In a new & more perfect Edition, Corrected and amended by the Author."

That's what is in store for you and for me and for all who have given themselves by faith to Jesus the Christ. We shall be changed. I believe in the resurrection of the body. Do you?

Amen.

# Chapter 14

# (I Believe in) the Life Everlasting

Text: Romans 6:18–23; Mark 10:17–22

In OT literature there are people who are hopeless and people who have picked up a glimpse of the something else that awaits those who trust God.

> Psalm 6:5 says, "For in death there is no remembrance of You; In the grave who will give you thanks?" Psalm 30:9 says, "What profit is there in my blood, when I go down to the pit? Will the dust praise You? Will it declare Your truth?"
>
> Psalm 88:10–12 then states, "Will You work wonders for the dead? Shall the dead arise and praise You? Shall Your lovingkindness be declared in the grave? Or Your faithfulness in the place of destruction? Shall Your wonders be known in the dark? And Your righteousness in the land of forgetfulness?"
>
> Psalm 39:13 says, "Remove Your gaze from me, that I may regain strength, before I go away and am no more." Isaiah 38:18 says, "For Sheol cannot thank You, Death cannot praise You; Those who go down

to the pit cannot hope for Your truth." Clearly these had no sense of a life that goes on forever.

J. E. McFadyen, an Old Testament scholar, says that this lack of a belief in immortality in the Old Testament is due to the power with which those men apprehended God in this world. He goes on to say, "There are few more wonderful things than this in the long story of religion, that for centuries men lived the noblest lives, doing their duties and bearing their sorrows, without hope of future reward; and they did this because in all their going out and coming in they were very sure of God."

There were, however, other writers in these same OT times who caught the vision of an afterlife. In Job 19:25–27, Job utters those words that we have used at funeral services. "I know that my Redeemer lives, And He shall stand at last on the earth; And after my skin is destroyed, this I know, that in my flesh I shall see God, whom I shall see for myself, and my eyes shall behold, and not another."

Similarly, the Moffatt Bible version of Job 19:25–27 says,

> Still, I know One to champion me at last,
> to stand up for me upon earth.
> This body may break up, but even then
> my life shall have a sight of God.

> Psalm 16:9–11 says, "Therefore my heart is glad, and my glory rejoices; My flesh also will rest in hope. For You will not leave my soul in Sheol, nor will You allow Your Holy One to see corruption. You will show me the path of life; in Your presence is fulness of joy; at Your right hand are pleasures for evermore."

> Psalm 73:24 says, " You will guide me with Your counsel, and afterward receive me to glory."

We have heard words of hopelessness and words of hopefulness. We believe that there *is* more to be experienced after death. We believe that the grave is not the end. If that were so, life would take on a different slant.

In the movie *The Casualties of War*, Michael J. Fox plays the role of a soldier in Vietnam who is part of a squad that rapes a young Vietnamese girl. Fox's character did not participate in the crime. Fox's character says to the men, "Just because each of us might at any second be blown away, we're acting like we can do anything we want, as though it doesn't matter what we do. I'm thinking it's just the opposite. Because we might be dead in the next split second, maybe we gotta be extra careful what we do. Because maybe it matters more. Maybe it matters more than we ever know."

If there were no consequences for our actions, we might all become rapists, robbers, rebels, or rascals. We might all live with no moral compass, no sense that we must give account for the deeds done in our bodies.

There *are* consequences, and there *is* something after this life. Offered to us in Jesus, we have life everlasting. Life everlasting is a statement of both duration *and* quality. It is the life that lasts long, *and* it is a certain *kind* of life. In John 10:10, Jesus said that He came to give life and that (life) more abundantly. That is, there is *life*, and then there is *abundant* life.

We also have the definition of life everlasting, which Jesus articulates in His high priestly prayer in John 17:3, which says, "And this is eternal life, that they may know You, the only true God, and Jesus Christ whom You have sent."

In our gospel lesson text, a young man approaches Jesus and asks a question about life everlasting. "What do I have to do in order to inherit eternal life?" he asks. Jesus tells him he must divest himself of his stuff and his attitude. The text says that he went away in great sorrow because he was wealthy (v. 22). Augustus Toplady's hymn "Rock of Ages" says, "Nothing in my hand I bring. Simply to Thy cross I cling." We can bring nothing to

Jesus that would increase our standing before Him—unless that something is a repentant, contrite heart. Life everlasting is not something we *achieve*. It is a gift we *receive* (Romans 6:23).

When I was a college student, I was visiting the home of a wealthy friend. He took me to a car dealership and said, "I want to buy you a car. I don't like the thought of your driving in the car you have." At the time I was a driving a car that was held together by prayer, rubber bands, and duct tape. After Clifford David Johnson gave me that newer car, it would have been silly of me to say, "Thanks for the gift. Now how much do I owe you?" A gift cannot be paid for by the receiver. When I was sixteen years old, my mother, knowing my love of classical music, gave me a beautiful box set of the complete *Messiah* by G. F. Handel. It would have been silly of me to say, "Mom, thanks for the gift. What do I owe you?"

C. S. Lewis wrote, "Christianity asserts that every individual human being is going to live forever, and this must be either true or false. Now there are a good many things which would not be worth bothering about if I were going to live only seventy years, but which I had better bother about very seriously if I am going to live forever."

Maybe you are reading this chapter and have not bothered to give thought to this issue of life everlasting. If you were only going to live seventy or eighty years, fine. But you will live forever. The question is where. We used to sing this chorus during the invitation in some churches.

He that believeth
He that believeth
Hath everlasting life
He that believeth in the Father and the Son
Hath everlasting life

How do we practically accept or gain God's gift of life

everlasting? I offer the acronym CRY, which stands for the following:

Confess (1 John 1:9).
Repent (Acts 3:19).
Yield (Romans 6:13).

At a recent Bible conference where I preached, I hosted a question-and-answer session. One woman asked, "When you get to heaven, is there anybody you want to see first?" Then I was asked if I wanted to ask God questions when I got there. I responded, "All I want is to see Jesus. I want to thank Him for the life I've had, the salvation He gave, the person He made me." I want to thank Him for life everlasting. Hallelujah!

Thinking of the fullness and duration of this wonderful life, W. B. Hinson, a great preacher of a past generation, spoke from his own experience just before he died. He said,

> I remember a year ago when a doctor told me, "You have an illness from which you won't recover." I walked out to where I live five miles from Portland, Oregon, and I looked across at that mountain that I love. I looked at the river in which I rejoice, and I looked at the stately trees that are always God's own poetry to my soul. Then in the evening I looked up into the great sky where God was lighting His lamps, and I said, "I may not see you many more times, but Mountain, I shall be alive when you are gone; and River, I shall be alive when you cease running toward the sea; and Stars, I shall be alive when you have fallen from your sockets in the great down pulling of the material universe!"

I am happy to report that I shall be alive when the organ is no longer played. I will be alive after the piano becomes silent. I shall be alive after the flowers that decorate our sanctuary fade and die. I shall be alive after the fibers in the carpeting disintegrate.

John 10:28 says, "And I give them eternal life, and they shall never perish; neither shall anyone snatch them out of My hand." According to Jesus, life everlasting means life that lasts forever! Amen.

# Chapter 15

# Amen

Text: Nehemiah 8:1–6

The ancient Hebrew word *amen* means "It is true," "I agree," or "That's right." In the New Testament, the equivalent word is *verily* (meaning "of a truth"). We will often sing amen at the end of a hymn. We have just sung a great theological truth, and we affirm all that we've sung by singing, "Amen!" "God in three persons, blessed Trinity. Amen." Some of us are from worship traditions in which *amen* is never said aloud. Others are from traditions in which *amen* is said aloud after songs, readings of Scriptures, and even announcements. Let's review how *amen* is used.

## Amen as Affirmation

In the best use of the word, *amen* is a rousing personal or corporate affirmation. It is our decision to put an exclamation point on what we just heard (Revelation 5:13–14; 7:9–12). That's the reason I am personally not one who stands up and starts, "Let the church say *amen*," before anything substantive has been said. In Deuteronomy 27:11–26, the consequences of disobedience are articulated before Israel, and the refrain is *amen*. *Amen* is not a response we reserve for when we feel good. It's a response we use when we've heard what is true.

The Psalter is a collection of 150 psalms. We don't refer to chapters but individual psalms. The entire collection of 150 psalms is divided into five books. At the end four of the five books of the psalms, there is a doxology, an ascription of praise to God and an *amen.* Let me show it to you here.

- Book 1 (1–41): Psalm 41:13
- Book 2 (42–72): Psalm 72:18–19
- Book 3 (73–89): Psalm 89:52
- Book 4 (90–106): Psalm 106:48
- Book 5 (107–150): Psalms 146–150

The *amen* here is the phrase "Praise the Lord," with which Psalms 146–150 begin. (See also 1 Chronicles 16:36.) In our text in Nehemiah 8, the Israelites have been released from captivity, and they have returned to the Holy City, Jerusalem. In this worship setting in chapter 8, Ezra the scribe retrieves the book of the law, and it is read from morning to midday (v. 3). Ezra was a prepared teacher of the law (Ezra 7:6, 10). The people's ears were attentive (Nehemiah 8:3). They heard the words of the law and vocally affirmed it, lifting up their hands (Nehemiah 8:6). Derek Kidner writes, "This day was to prove a turning point. From now on, the Jews would be predominantly 'a people of the book.'"

## Amen as Aspiration

Sometimes we say *amen* to that which is not yet understood by us. It is not yet embraced by us. However, what has been said is that to which we aspire. Perhaps that is where some are with the Apostles' Creed. Maybe you do not yet fully believe in Jesus Christ, who was conceived by the Holy Ghost, born of the Virgin Mary, suffered under Pontius Pilate, was crucified, died, and was buried. Maybe you are not convinced that He rose from the dead on the third day and ascended into heaven. Maybe for you the creed is what you *want* to believe. You are like the man in Mark 9, whose son was given to seizures and convulsions. After Jesus declared that all things were possible to the person who believes, the father of the boy said, "Lord, I believe; help my unbelief" (Mark 9:24).

Let us avoid using *amen* as an affectation. Let it not be frivolously thrown around. Instead, let us affirm what God has said and done with a great *amen*.

God has created the heavens and the earth. Amen. God has sent us Jesus Christ, His only Son, our Lord. Amen. Jesus was conceived by the Holy Ghost, born of the Virgin Mary, suffered under Pontius Pilate, was crucified, died, and was buried. Amen. Christ rose from the dead. Amen. Christ ascended into heaven and sits at God's right hand. Amen. He is coming to judge the living and the dead. Amen. God sent us the Holy Ghost. Amen. He called us into the holy Christian family of God, which is called the Church. Amen. God has provided the forgiveness of sins though Christ and the resurrection of the body, and He has given us life everlasting. Amen!

In the creed we have a set of organized, well-articulated doctrinal statements. Amen. Finally we have Christ Himself who, according to Revelation 3:14, is the *amen*. In the words of one writer, Christ is the "Amen Substantive" (The Biblical Illustrator. Nehemiah. p. 110). He is the affirmation of God. The Apostles' Creed closes with *amen*. So does our Bible. The revealed Word of God, to which we hold fast, closes with this: "The grace of our Lord Jesus Christ be with you all" (Revelation 22:21).

Amen.